do they make coffins that small?
ministry in an age of uncertainty

We're not good at death these days. Don't like Crow. Death was never without trauma, but in the past we had rituals to prop us up. Now we're alone. Ali Sangster's vivid stories, often killingly (!) funny, are rooted in our shared earthiness and hint at the rumour of God. You'll find this wee book a page-turner and maybe a life-turner, too.

Rev. Dr Peter Matheson
widely published religious historian

While not a Methodist herself, Alex's life has serendipitously involved Methodist clergy showing up in pivotal ways on several occasions. My writing of these words may be yet another. There's an old saying from the States back in the era of the circuit riders who rode from town to town on horseback, "This weather's only fit for crows and Methodist preachers!" The weather in which Alex Sangster's book *Do they make coffins that small?* Arrives – isn't good.

The literal climate is experiencing the increasing impact of global warming; and the societal climate is one that has become quite opposed to organised religion in general, and Christianity in particular.

This book is one that transcends genres. It is part memoir and part theo-poetics and it employs the tool of magical realism. The reader is artfully guided from present, to past, to future, to present; and from actual accounts to poetic interpretation – like a river that simultaneously flows in multiple directions, and yet doesn't leave us dizzy, but, instead, seeing more clearly than ever.

In her book, we encounter slices of Alex's personal and professional life – especially her unexpected falling in love with the way of Jesus, her call to ordained ministry, and profound instances of pastoral life where the rubber hits the road. She has us co-experiencing moments of interacting with gravediggers, grieving parents of an infant who died; to being arrested by an officer who receives pastoral care from the person she is arresting. Think James Harriot's *All Creatures*, sharing of the rich and varied life of a Yorkshire veterinarian, meets Carlos Fuentes' *The Old Gringo* and John Nichols' *The Milagro Beanfield War*.

This lovely book is easy on the eye, a delight to read, and is a powerful apologetic that helps us fathom why at least some people are choosing to swim against the societal current and follow that bold and compassionate soul from Nazareth.

Roger Wolsey
author, Kissing Fish: Christianity for People Who Don't Like Christianity;
and Discovering Fire: Spiritual Practices That Transform Lives.

What a brilliant book – its empathy, honesty, imagery, style, language and commitment. In beautiful prose, Alexandra Sangster invites us into her life and calling with whimsy and depth, through snippets of reflection, conversations, grief and hope. It will be loved by fellow clergy who will identify; progressives who see her devotion to people in spite of the church; by those who ask "Why be a minister"; by those who have cared for the homeless and destitute; and for those who have watched loved ones die. Be prepared to be touched and inspired.

Dr Val Webb
theologian and author

Raw and captivating. The words and imagery, as in the title, will grip you. You will either not be able to put the book down, or not be able to absorb it in one sitting, as your spirit allows. Powerful.

Dr Carl Krieg
author of *What to Believe? the Questions of Christian Faith*,
The Void and the Vision
and *The New Matrix: How the World We Live In Impacts Our Thinking About Self and God*

Glorious and moving, ordinary and extraordinary in equal measure – these are poems of profound perspicacity, found at that edge where life meets the biggest questions of all.

Georgia Richter
Publisher, Fremantle Press

To my mother – who taught me to see the beauty.
And to my father – who believed in me, utterly.
Vale.

And to my created family, who are numinous with life.
I love you.

The author respectfully acknowledges the Wurundjeri peoples who are the custodians of the unceded land on which this book was written. Always was, always will be.

do they make coffins that small?

ministry in an age of uncertainty

alexandra sangster

Published in Australia by
Coventry Press
33 Scoresby Road
Bayswater VIC 3153

ISBN 9781922589378

Copyright © Alexandra Sangster 2023

All rights reserved. Other than for the purposes and subject to the conditions prescribed under the *Copyright Act*, no part of this publication may be reproduced, stored in a retrieval system, or transmitted in any form or by any means, electronic, mechanical, photocopying, recording or otherwise, without the prior permission of the publisher.

Catalogue-in-Publication entry is available from the National Library of Australia
http://catalogue.nla.gov.au

Cover design by Ian James – www.jgd.com.au
Text design by Coventry Press
Set in EB Garamond

Printed in Australia

table of contents

introduction	11
the calling	11
saying yes	12
ancestors	14
a note on structure	15
a note on Crow (black bird, raven, merl, rook)	15
the gravedigger 1	18
the ashes	22
the call 1	28
the gravedigger 2	31
the crow 1	32
the pastoral visit 1	35
the crow 2	36
the world 1	37
the world 2	38
the world 3	39

ghosts 1	40
the hit and run 1	43
the assessment	45
the work 1	46
the work 2	49
the crow 3	54
the work 3	62
the work 4	63
the hit and run 2	65
the world 4	68
the pastoral visit 2	69
the gravedigger 3	70
the world 5	72
the world 6	73
the gravedigger 4	80
the work 5	84
the work 6	86
the world 7	88
the call 2	89

the work 7	91
the work 8	95
the call 3	99
the list	100
the work 9	103
the call 4	105
the work 10	106
the work 11	108
the call 5	112
the work 12	113
the work 13	116
the world 8	118
ghosts 2	119
the work 14	123
the work 15	124
the work 16	129
the gravedigger 5	138
Sources	147

Acknowledgments 148

do they make coffins that small – a radio play. 149

introduction

the calling

Not many people imagine that one day they will grow up to be an ordained minister.

I certainly didn't. The book that you are about to read opens a window into some of the specific, and for many, unknown, experiences of being a minister of religion.

What it is like to do a funeral?
Are you ready to sit with people in their darkest moments?
How do you grapple with a sense of call?
Can you be open to the mystical breaking through, into the everyday?

I was raised by socialist hippies up in Melbourne's Dandenong Ranges. Neither of them had anything to do with institutional religion, and both were scathing about the church. What my parents did believe in, though, was social justice and changing the world and I grew up knowing that this was what I had to do (no pressure).

One of the most common reactions I get from people, when they find out what I do, is shock and not just shock because I am a woman, or shock because I am under 95, but shock because their understanding of the Christian church is that it is a place of raging fundamentalism, racism, sexism and homophobia and so these folk – who don't know me – ask:

But how?
But why?
Why would you belong to an institution which is symbolic of all these things?
I was always aware, as a very small child, of God inside and around me.
Like a deep vibration,
like a blood, beat, hum,
there was a 'this-ness' to creation, which spoke to me, of a living spirit, immanent in the whole of life. Tree, rock, animal and bird – all were shot through with an energy that was theirs alone, but which was also connected, by invisible filaments, to a cosmic song, that we might call God.

saying yes

As I grew, this awareness of God didn't leave me, but the stories that I was told about God, I didn't understand. If God was all powerful, why was there so much suffering? And how could this God (whom I knew in my heart as deep and burning love) possibly have preordained the death of his son in some kind of weird sacrifice for the collective sins of a people born out of a fairytale Adam and Eve, who themselves had only 'sinned' because God had tempted them in the first place?

No, I didn't get the church.

So when I found myself called, called in a way both awe-full and mortifying, I did not even have a language to understand what this call was.

Absurd, ridiculous, embarrassing... I had not even been baptised. I was seeing at this time, a counsellor, a retired Methodist minister called Alf Foote and I told him what was happening and he, in his wisdom, sent me along to the Rev. Coralie Ling who was the minister at Fitzroy UCA, a radical feminist community. Eight years later, I was ordained.

At my ordination, I quoted the Archbishop of Canterbury, who said:

I was converted first, and spent the rest of my life working out the intellectual implications

and I also quoted Ted Hughes in one of his many poems about Crow.

Crow realised God loved him –
Otherwise, he would have dropped dead. So that was proved.
Crow reclined, marvelling, on his heartbeat.
And he realised that God spoke Crow – Just existing was His revelation.

ancestors

The Uniting Church in Australia that I was ordained into recognises that the same Spirit that is within Jesus, existed here, with the First Peoples, before the colonisers came. What this means is that the church I said 'Yes' to says 'Yes' to a theology that is progressive, expansive and radical.

It would've been much easier and cooler if I had not been called to be a Christian minister – people would've been very accepting if I had become a Buddhist Nun or a Whirling Dervish, or a follower of Wicca, but the hound of heaven hunted me down through the years, and I felt in my own body the crucifixion and resurrection of the one whom we know as love. I don't believe that Jesus is the only way to God (I think that Jesus is one of many) but, ancestrally, his story is mine.

My hope for this book is that, for people of faith, you will find courage and consolation in these pages, and you will also, perhaps, find moments of connection into some of the deepest and most sacred work that clergy are called to do. For people outside of this ancient story, folk who are spiritually hungry but anti-institution, my hope is that you will feel a softening and an opening to the possibility that faith stories may well be part of what knits the cosmos together.

a note on structure

do they make coffins that small? employs a symphonic method of scoring memories (like discordant and harmonising notes) side by side. The reader is invited to embrace a nonlinear narrative and to follow multiple threads of a vocational journey.

Let the titles act as cairns on the map. Time loops back on itself and the story makes its nest in memory. We are always at the beginning and the middle and the end.

a note on Crow (black bird, raven, merl, rook)

Sometimes being a minister feels like being a crow.

Both crows and ministers embody stories of darkness, death, communication and connection. Neither is neutral in people's minds. Both evoke strong emotional responses which are not personal to the individual crow or clergy.

Across cultures, there have always been people set apart to become vessels of spirit. The name changes – shaman, priest, iman, mystic or rabbi – but their role – to communicate with the sacred and to care for souls – is the same. Similarly, across cultures, crows have always been endowed with story.

They are: harbingers of doom, night walkers, they have a claw in each world, they are messengers between the living and the dead, they sit on the shoulders of the Gods and whisper secrets about sorrow.

Crows follow me wherever I go.

They call at me when I am preaching (sometimes so loudly that neither I nor the congregation can hear a word that I am saying). They hop at my feet as I bury the dead, they swoop over my head as I ride across the city, and they follow my gaze as I walk down by the Yarra. People look at us both with horror, we symbolise death and we sit with bodies and watch the spirit passing.

Within many First Peoples belief systems, including the Celts from who my bloodline runs, there are ideas about particular animals with whom humans may have a spiritual connection.

This idea – sometimes called animism – recognises that there is a spirit within all living things – including plants and earth – which can be experienced and honoured and can connect us into a bigger conversation that just our own human one. The Bible is rich with images of God as one who is manifest in fire and light and cloud and who creates each animal as sentient and each with a soul that sings. Crow has been, and is, my companion in my call. From Crow I get courage and community and a reminder that all of us are in this living and dying thing, together.

the gravedigger 1

He is waist-high in orange mud,
leaning on the shovel and squinting at the sky.
The cemetery is silent, apart from the sound of his breath.
And mine.

How long you been doing this for?
What, shovelling?
Nah, grave-digging.
Oh yeah, oh well, ten? Ten to fifteen years?
Do you like it?
Yeah, yeah, it's good eh, you're outdoors, pretty much your own boss.
Tell ya what an' all, I'm everyone's mate at parties.
Really?
Oh yeah, everyone wants to hear the stories.
That's weird, no one wants to hear my stories.
Really?
Yeah, I think it's like I'm like death or something, like death to them, or I might try and convert them.
Yeah no one wants that, eh.
Nah, no one.

A crow cracks the sky with a sharp shout of cawwwww and I startle and then call back, it's something I've been doing for so long that I barely notice the flicker of a question mark on the gravedigger's face.

Crows
I say, as way of explanation.
He nods at me and then begins to shovel again.

Mostly, gravediggers use an auger for shoveling out the earth. An auger is a machine made up of a spiraling metal shaft and its name comes from the ancestor of the old English word for spear – *nafogar*. In my mind's eye, I see the gravedigger, silhouetted against the sun and instead of his raised shovel, a spear, pointed at dark earth.

Mostly too, they don't dig down the 6 feet deep of old chanting children's rhymes, but instead only 4 feet. Of course, when multiple family members are buried in the same grave, the 6 feet is necessary as it allows for stacking, one coffin atop of another. The 6 feet deep tradition traces its origins back to a clutch of dark stories. Some believe it started around the time of the Black Death of 1665 when the City of London swam thick with the plague. A pamphlet was released by the Court of Aldermen and the Lord Mayor entitled 'Burial of the Dead' which was published in the hope that if the citizens followed these instructions – including burying the dead 6 feet down, so the plague held in their bodies could not escape – it could be a way to stop the spread. Another theory holds that 6 foot was the average height of a man and so to dig deeper would make it harder to get out once the job had been done, and yet another theory focused on 6 feet being the best way to avoid disturbance of the corpse by animals or robbers.

The family have begun to assemble, awkwardly getting out of the cars which have followed the hearse. Women ease dresses out of underpants, where they have creviced in the drive, men adjust themselves in too small suits, none of them want to be here. This is a foreign country and they do not know the language and they didn't book the tickets and yet, here they are. Sometimes I feel like I should be holding a scythe, better to usher them over the river. Instead, I help them navigate the still-wet earth, leading them along the edges of the old graves, so they can avoid stepping on the heads of the long dead, and then get them to gather close enough so they can hear me, without farcical yelling.
And then I begin

So, we gather here,
with NN but not with him
His body is here,
so precious
the bones, the blood
the settling into
the body which is now empty of spirit,
empty of that burning spark which filled his eyes with grace
and his lungs with breath
and so we say goodbye
in our mind's eye
to this body
and together we commit his earthly remains to the elements
oh mystery of eternal love
We commend to you your child NN

the gravedigger 1

Now that he has passed from this mortal life
and we join with
the ancients of earth
and the choirs of angels
in releasing him home
to you

A small boy in front of me is weeping, he can't stop, his father grips his shoulder but doesn't seem to be able to help, he too is crying and seems incapable of comforting his boy.
I stop, I walk over, I bend down.

It hurts, doesn't it?
yes
It's ok that it hurts.
That's love, what your feeling, that's your heart breaking and that's ok.

He looks at me, slightly aghast and then seems to understand and then he begins to cry even more. I stay on my knees, in my Alb, in the dirt, for just a little while longer, long enough for him to know that his grief isn't scary and then I return to burying his grandpa.

Cawwwwwwwww

the ashes

The room is small with one coffin and one cupboard. It smells like sand, like dust, like cheap candles. In front of me, leaning against the wall, there are rows of tiny houses, made of what looks like tin. The houses are heaped at awkward angles.

It is the aftermath of an earthquake,
the ground has cracked,
and they are the survivors, but they are teetering on the edge.

I know about these tiny houses. Last time I was here to do a funeral, I had asked the funeral director, him with the slicked back hair and the three-piece suit:

What's with the little houses?

Houses? Oh, you mean the candle boxes? It's for the Greeks, they light the candles you know, for the dead.

Later, I look them up and discover that in the orthodox tradition each grave has its own little house to sit on top of the marble, with a lit candle within and it burns for forty days and forty nights. Just the same amount of time, apparently, that Jesus was running free in the wilderness after his baptism, taunted and tempted by the Darkness, and fed on hope and honey by the Light. Apparently, the burning candle inside the tiny house is meant to symbolise a vigil of constant prayer for the deceased. I wonder if, by lighting the candle, the family feel that their work is done or if they, also, pray and if so, what they pray for? Intercessory prayer has never made any sense to me. Either God is love or God is not and certainly God has no power, or at least not in the bolt of lightning kind of way, this much seems abundantly clear...

think tsunami, think holocaust, think mother birthing in bombed-out cellar, think every day random tumour, think child stepping off tram, think speeding car, think...

abyss

My research reveals to me that one local company has designed a special little house made of Colorbond with a Perspex window,
to stand strong,
under the Aussie sun.
And that in Alaska, the Athabascan First Peoples who were colonised by orthodox missionaries have created their own version
tiny colourful wooden cottages, painted in the colours of the family,
placed on the graves as a wee spirit house,
for the ubiquitous forty days and forty nights that the soul is roaming
the earth,
before facing up to the final judgment.

I wonder if
sometimes
the souls decide to just hide,
inside the houses
and not come out?
How nice it would be to visit
to peer through the tiny windows and watch them going about their days
making soup on tiny stoves and reading poetry by the fire.

Ahem, good to go in ten?

It's the funeral director again, his head popping through the door.

Yes
(Shit, the Reading, I forgot to bring the Reading)
I start flicking through my phone trying to find something appropriate online.
Once again, I have forgotten to bring a Bible and the funeral is about to begin.
The cupboard... maybe inside the cupboard there will be a Bible.
I pull open the door and inside on the shelves there are stacks upon stacks
of small
black
boxes.
Not like the ones made of tin, these are cardboard and rectangular and faded, and I wonder if they are pianola rolls and if they are,
then why are they here?
The funeral director ducks his head back in from behind the curtain. He watches me staring into his cupboard.

Ahem, just checking, shall we close the coffin?

I nod, yes, the family have had the viewing, the wax face of their mother with the too blue eyeshadow and the now thin lips has been kissed or patted. There has been warm flesh on cold and the warm has recoiled, instinctual and then guilty. I know this interaction, between the living and the dead. I have watched it play out, over and over again.

Yes.. um.. what's with the pianola rolls?

They are ashes.
Ashes?
Yes, left behind, the families never come, we don't know what to do with them, and we can't throw them away, so...
Box upon box, life upon life, all tucked up in the dark.
I wonder if they talk to each other.

Been here long?
Years and years – what about you?
I just moved – from the cupboard down the hall.
Alive long?
3 score and 10
Like in the Bible?
Yes and you?
Oh I died young... I did think that they would miss me...
Well, maybe their hearts were too broken,
or they all moved away?
Yeah, maybe...
away...
so here I am...

I wonder if they tut to each other or quarrel, quietly.
Or maybe there is simply silence,
and cardboard
and dust
and bone.

the ashes

The funeral director coughs; he is one of twins and I never know who is who.

Death looks at me from the conveyer belt in my mind, his knees are tucked up and he is checking his watch.

Are you good to go?

Yes.

I walk out with the coffin,
a brand-new death.
Not yet in a box, on the shelf. Not yet.

the call 1

Minister: c. 1300,
Medieval Latin,
meaning
'priest'
from minus, minor
meaning
'less' or 'little'
originally
'to serve'.
So, I am called to be little and less and to act with the authority of another and to serve. It's not your usual job description.
Yet here I am.
I am kneeling on dark green carpet.
They are laying their hands upon my head. The air all around me is humming, iridescent.
Numinous, almost liquid – it glows from within itself.
And as I kneel,
and as time stands still,
I find myself wondering, yet again, how I ended up here.
Here being 'here'
specifically
on my knees
in a church.

We give you thanks that you have called (insert name here) whom we ordain in your name.

we pray that the holy spirit will endow (him/her) with grace and power
be of good courage
hold fast to that which is good.
Render no one evil for evil...

The church is full, an ordination is always an event.
Earlier, I stood, in the dusty half-light of evening, outside my one-hundred-year-old red brick Methodist church, surrounded by other ministers, all dressed in white. We were waiting to process in, waiting for the congregation to stand and sing, voices swelling and carrying me down, to the altar.
The other ministers milled around, Albs flapping, red stoles like fire. You don't get to wear a stole until you are ordained. Mine is waiting for me in the church,
bright
blood
red
and hand sewed with tiny stitches.

There is no one origin story for why clergy wear stoles. Some believe it is a symbol of the yoke that Christ spoke of when he told his friends to follow him. A yoke is the frame that connects two animals together. So to be 'yoked' is to be joined to another, usually in an act of servitude. I wonder who I am being yoked to? In the gospels, Jesus encourages those who are 'heavy laden' to take his yoke upon them, and in so doing they will find rest for their souls. Presumably this was because Jesus was trying to do away with theologies of legalism and self-righteousness and the oppressive rules of the colonising empire and so this is why he claimed that his 'yoke was easy and his burden light'. It doesn't feel light, in this moment.

My heart is thudding.
electric,
every cell in me
aflame.
Bigger than my wedding day. Nothing gentle or familiar, like stepping off a cliff.

Inside the church, my husband and my baby daughter are waiting. Inside are all the people I have vowed to care for. Inside is over 2000 years of Christian history. Inside is a young man, only a few years older than me, but dead now, of course,

yet
resurrected
and all
aglow
sitting, with a crow,
on his lap.

The procession surges, up the stone steps and into the church, the people stand and sing.
It is begun.

the gravedigger 2

Do you know some people lie in graves overnight?
Nah, that's not legal.
No, not a real grave, just one they dig themselves.
Why would ya wanna do that?
It's like a spiritual thing, like contemplating death, or something.
Sounds stupid to me... and I'm always shoveling thru bugs. I wouldn't want one of those in my ear. What about you but, you must have some good stories eh?
Yeah, I've got a few.
Like what?
Um like the time I was doing the funeral, you know at the graveside.
and the widower, he came up to me,
just as I'm inviting everyone to pray,
and he gives me a can of tuna –
to keep my strength up.
What did you do?
Well... I took it and I ate it, I ate it later, it was kind of moving actually.
Yeah.
Yeah.

the crow 1

crow realised that God loved him
so that was proved and crow realised that god spoke crow:
just existing was his revelation (Ted Hughes)

Crow: part of the corvid mob,
magpies, rooks, jays, jackdaws,
ravens
(the biggest
the blackest,
their name comes from the Latin rapere:
the act of tearing)
Crow: their beaks are engraved on the doorsteps of early
British churches
to remind the locals
of how the Vikings
once nailed the Christians,
to the doors.
Crow: apparently one fed,
one of
the Desert Fathers
bread,
for 60 years,
appearing every day
like a
falling
black
star.

And, of course, there was Elijah, the Hebrew Prophet, who was led by Yahweh into the wild, a crow was his companion, feeding him twice a day.
Crow: In Victoria, he's called 'Waa'.
Crow: In Arnhem land, he's 'Wak', the younger brother of Bungil the eagle,
burnt black by fire.
Crow: In Scotland, she is war goddess
Her name is 'Badb Catha'
She is
battle crow.
In Victoria, the state where I live, we don't have crows – only ravens. But in Australia we have the Little Raven, the Little Crow, the Forest Raven, and the Torresian Crow.
When they are young, crows are called:
nestlings
and they have blue eyes
and if they are lucky enough to survive their first 2 years
(most don't)
then they can live up to 30 years.

Crow: harbinger of doom, night walker, one claw in each world, messenger.
Crow: they mourn their dead, they partner for life,
their call
cuts across the cumulus cloud
and brick building and back lots
with overflowing bins
where they tear chicken carcasses
apart.

Do they make coffins that small?

Crow: everywhere I go, they are, watching
Crow: Sometimes on a Sunday they caterwaul so loudly that no one can hear me preach,
I open my mouth and out comes:
Waaaaaaaaaaaaaaaaaaaaaaa

the pastoral visit 1

I am standing at the door.
I am knocking on the door.
I think it's the right address,
given to me by the funeral home.
I am knocking.
Yes?
I am the minister; I've come about the...
Minister, we don't need a minister, no one needs a minister here, no!
She slams the door shut.
In my face.
waawaaaaaaaaaaaaaaaaaaaaaa

the crow 2

Crow: Apollo's bird, Word of God.
Crow: Odin's' bird, two brothers called Memory and Reflection,
they whisper in the Norse God's ear,
then fly off,
to be:
blood drinker,
corpse dancer

Minister, we don't need a minister, no one needs a minister here, no!

People once believed that when someone died,
a crow would carry their soul to the land of the dead.
But sometimes, something so bad had happened,
that there was a terrible
sadness
and the soul couldn't rest.
Then sometimes, just sometimes,
the crow could bring that soul back, to put the wrong things right.

the world 1

I didn't grow up wanting to be a minister but a minister I am.
That sentence alone is a strange enough.
When I was little and as I grew older,
if I thought about ministers at all, which I rarely ever did, I thought of old robed men from a medieval world of conservatism and cardigans.
Like on the BBC, in a village:
Well, yes, Mrs Highton, but as you can see the Lord does not feel that way.
We did not go to church as a family not even in a Christmas and Easter kind of way.
It was simply,
an irrelevance.

the world 2

So, wait – does that mean you believe in God?

The party is a kaleidoscope of bass beats, smoke, dense air and warm bodies, pressed up close and on the move. He is yelling into my ear. I am plummeting internally. I have had this conversation so many times. It usually goes like this:

So, what are you studying?
Theology.
What's that?
'Theo' from 'god', so like, the study of God.
Oh cool like all the gods, like Thor and Buddha and stuff?
Actually, just Christianity.
Oh god – why!
I'm training to be a minister.
What, like a priest with a church? Will you, like, preach sermons and shit?
Woah – why the hell would you want to do that?

the world 3

Atheists across time have long argued that religion is:
the opiate of the masses
and that only the truly feeble-brained
and emotionally stunted of us
would cling to the idea that this
reality
is not all there is.
Just accept the inevitable, die and be done
they say
Stop being like a child crying in the dark
they say.
Stop cuddling up,
to your imaginary friend.
But a saint once said:
Here is the world.
Beautiful and terrible things will happen.
Do not be afraid.

ghosts 1

Do you believe in ghosts, Gran?
No, don't be ridiculous.
I've seen your grandfather a few times.
He's a ball of white light flashing around the room.
I say:
Tom, Tom, is that you?
And then he's gone.
And sometimes he'll hop into bed with me,
I'll wake up and all the covers are gone, and I'll say:
Tom, Tom, move over.
No, I don't believe in ghosts.
I just know what I know.

This was the same Gran who, after a major car accident lay,
medically dead
on a bed,
in the hospital
and
who watched
from the upper right corner of the room
as the medical staff slipped quietly into emergency mode,
and declared her gone,
and then brought her back to life.
Who then saw her mother and father and older sister Elsie,
(the one who had fallen, fitting, from an apple tree when she
was a girl)
standing in a green field and waving to her,

but who knew that she still had work to do,
and so,
with great reluctance,
came rushing back, into the
broken,
body,
on the bed.

Families are full of stories like my Gran's.
I hear them all the time.
Stories of premonitions and of dreams and of the figures of
dead fathers, standing,
at the foot of the bed.
Stories that go like this:
I saw a wren, just like she loved, it hopped right towards me.
Or like this:
I heard his name in my head and then I got the call.
Or like this:
**I saw her in the doorway, and she smiled at me, and that's
when I knew –
she was gone.**
Or this:
**He came and sat with me, and he held me,
and it was all really normal,
but then I remembered,
he was dead.**
Or even:
**She was with me – it was a dream, I know that, but when I
woke, for the first time it was like, I knew I would survive this,
because she was gone,
but she was here,**

if you know what I mean.
Or this one:
I was going into the woods to end it all, I had the rope around my neck and then the deer came, it stood right in front of me. Staring.
I knew it was her,
so I put down the rope.
And of course:
I felt them on my chest. I was lying down and they both sort of sat on my chest and hugged me and it was so warm and weird that they were together because they never were, when they were alive, but here they both were, sitting on me and I cried and cried and cried.

Stories of friends visiting,
like a glance in the mind,
and then the phone –
ringing.

the hit and run 1

Cast

Brian: Old Australian, stepped straight out of the pages of Patrick White's
Tree of Man.
Sees God in his own spit,
hanging off the gum branch.
Loves motorbikes, has a whole shed of them,
posts parts to people all over Australia.
Very,
very tall, a tree,
walking.

Craig: Dead at 28. Worked as a ghost in a jail, loved his brothers,
went to church on Saturday nights,
knew all the words to Bob Dylan's 'Hurricane'.
Taller than his dad.
Sitting at the traffic lights on his motorbike,
then comes the kid in a stolen car.
160k per hour. For a moment, before he hit the road,
Craig
flew.

Jayne: The girlfriend.

Ali: Me.

Scene: Interior house, night, dark corridor,
FX: sound of phone ringing, enter Ali.

>> She picks up phone.
>> V/O Brian speaks...

Brian: **Is Jayne there?**

Ali: *No, no, she's not here; I think she was staying at Craig's house. Is everything all right?*

Brian: No, Ali, no, this is Brian, everything is not all right. Brian, Craig's dad, everything is not all right. Craig has been killed, love.

Stage Direction: Ali falls and opens her mouth.
No sound comes out.
The silent cry.
She stumbles down the darkened corridor.
She bangs on doors,
She begins to yell.

Ali: *WAKE UP! WAKE UP! WAKE UP!*

the assessment

So, you are here today for your psychiatric assessment for the ministry.
We want you to hear the voice of God but not be hearing voices, you know what I mean, heh heh, just my little joke, don't be nervous, let's start with your mother shall we?
Tell me about your mother...

Later, as I'm walking home along the shoreline of one of Melbourne's tired bays, I can feel the outrage flapping, bat-like, in my mind. That I have been examined, dissected and unravelled. It begins to rain and the sand beneath my feet is littered with all the lost plastic crap of the world and despairs fills me.

What a stupid thing, stupid, stupid!

To be a minister, to say 'yes' to this claustrophobic and conflicted church, to be surrounded by culturally conservative caregivers, to step into a horror story from history, all those institutions, all that abuse. I start to run, breath ragged, tears and rain on face, running on sand sucks and I stagger, and I fall. I call my mum and she laughs and I think maybe she's happy – to have been the source of so much examination.

Come home.
She tells me,
Come home and tell me all about it.

the work 1

I spend my days at a Drop In. It was birthed over 40 years ago by a congregation wanting to feed the hungry and house the homeless. Over the years, it has gone through multiple renovations, stepping into shinier new skins and under different funding models, but the heart of her remains the same. You come here when you have nowhere else to go.

You come here and have breakfast and lunch and do your laundry and have a shower. You come here and people know your name. Drop Ins are not popular anymore. It's all about individual support packages and engaging as a consumer.

(But then Jesus, in the Gospel story, smashes the tables in the temple and yells: GET OUT! GET OUT!)

Our Drop In needs constant defending from a world that wants 'engagement' and 'results' but we all know that the biggest killer is loneliness.
Everybody knows.
As Mother Teresa (that grumpy, holy, frightened, human saint) once said:
'The biggest disease today is not leprosy or cancer or tuberculosis, but rather the feeling of being unwanted, uncared for and deserted – by everybody'.

the work 1

At the Drop In, I sing, and I dance, and I clean the floor,
and I hold people's hands and I am hugged,
all the time
and I wash the dishes and sometimes I wash bodies.

At the Drop In, we share communion, in a way that is raw and ragged and utterly filled with joy. I hold up the bread and people fall to their knees and begin to weep. Here, more than anywhere else (except perhaps the dementia wards and hospices where the bread is taken without even a hint,
of a veil between this world and the next and the hands are sometimes too weak
or lost to hold themselves out,
so I put the bread
directly into their mouths,
like a mother bird
like a crow –
feeding
a saint).

At the Drop In, prayers are prayed for:
no more bedbugs
and no more smack
and no more temptation
and no more lack,
of love,
and we laugh,
like drains
and sing songs – spirituals are best,
and we pray for the world, from all our poverty, in our little circle, around a single candle and the prayers are so heartfelt,

that even I, with all my progressive theology
think that maybe, just maybe,
they might come true.

the work 2

We are but dust and ashes.
He says the words with me,
he stumbles over the ash.
in his mouth.
I have got down on my knees in front of him and so he,
thinking this is part of the ritual, gets down on his knees too,
I anoint with ash,
a sign of the cross on his
very
human
brow.

Moments before, another man, all hennaed hair and tattoos of
Jesus,
had been telling me,
about spiritual emergencies
and about how
once,
I became a diamond,
trapped in space.
and how he thought,
that
maybe
I would never escape.
but that slowly,
he found his way back,
into his body again.

We are but dust and ashes.
An older woman begins to speak,
she is wrapped in blankets,
(even though it is not cold)
and she pulls them tight as she remembers,
an Ash Wednesday
from long ago
where the sky rained floating trees from burning bush
in hills
and how
when folk were leaving the church
it was like
snow,
but hot,
on our faces.
Later, on a visit, I hear about
the aneurism
and of how
I was all alone,
and of how
God once came into my kitchen,
and it was all,
aglow
Dark outside, you know... but inside... the light... I had asked
for help you see.
Meanwhile on this day, in Australia, there is a flood.
The water won't stop rising,
and in the Ukraine
there is a war,
raging.
My kneeling man begins to weep and the church fills with his
soft animal sighs.

This is my first Ash Wednesday service in this church, and I had opened the doors to anyone who wanted to come, expecting no one, but in they came, the rough sleepers, the man who lives in the bush out the front of the building and the participants at the Drop In. Earlier that day, I had stood in the dining area, in my Alb (the long white priests robe that I wear when I am leading worship, named Alb after the Latin *albus* – for white – the colour in which all other colours become one) spruiking the service, like a medieval salesman:

Any one for ash?
Come and get your ash for Ash Wednesday!

What's Ash Wednesday?
yells back one of the participants.
Fair enough. I had no idea either before I started studying theology all those years ago. The first Ash Wednesday rituals were held sometime in the 11th century, a time in Europe of battling Popes and Kings and nobody really knows how or why it first started.
What we do know is that
ash
is dead fire,
the opposite of life.
We do know that God, in one of the many origin stories of humanity,
tells Adam and Eve to:
'*Remember you that you are dust, and to dust you shall return*'
when banish.
ing them from the garden
and we do know.

that on this day we are asked to remember our mortality.
To be humble,
to be humus
(of the earth)
and to literally smear that earth
on our foreheads,
so we can't forget.

Of course, the ashes used on Ash Wednesday are meant to be made, not from dirt, but from the ash of the burnt palm branches kept from the previous year's Palm Sunday services – Palm Sunday being the Sunday immediately before Easter Sunday. Palm Sunday being the day where Jesus engages in an awesome piece of street theatre propaganda,
and enters the city,
at the time of Passover
riding on a donkey, at exactly the same time that the Roman governor of Judea rides up to Jerusalem, with his soldiers and his cavalry to reinforce the imperial garrison in Jerusalem and to proclaim the pomp and power of empire. This procession of Jesus is about justice and the end of violence. It's about community and humility and it's about dancing.
Children and adults
dressed in rags,
and dancing.

So, the palm branches are meant to be burnt and blessed – often by sprinkling holy water on them – and then mixing them with oil, to stop them from flying away.
Every year, this part of the ritual sees me frantically looking for the dusty box of last year's crosses (made from the palm leaves

we waved in the procession) which I have stashed somewhere on a shelf in whatever church I happen to be in and then crumbling them up, to attempt to burn them enough to make ash, but not so much that they burn into nothing. This is trickier than it sounds, and I often wonder why no one gives us lessons on this at minister school and how, it seems, that we are just meant to know what to do.

My man is still weeping.
Up you get, Stevie, up you get.

I hold out my hands and he falls into them, I am enveloped in a fug of the unwashed, of cheap, sour wine and salty water. I dance him upright, an awkward waltz of steadying.
These times, these biblical times.

the crow 3

waaaa waaa waaa waaaaaaaaaaaaa

Crow comes with me to the funeral of my friend Margaret.
Literally, he is there.
He is always there.
Crow hops on one claw.

Going to visit people who are dying is kind of part of the drill, like core business.
Hatches, matches, dispatches – that's what we do.
I was told by a professor at Theological Hall.
And so I do, I visit.

Sometimes there is fluid. Like tears and sweat and all the other outpourings that seep and flow and flood from our breaking bodies. Sometimes I hold hands or take off bras or remove sheets. Sometimes they vomit and apologise and weep and together we wipe and settle back.

Smooth the dying pillow.

Sometimes they are sleeping and part of my brain curses because I will have to come back and see them again and, actually, I am crazy busy and I don't know how I will find the time before they die and then I feel dreadful because,

when they finally open their eyes,
I am
so
grateful
that I get to bless them and to thank them and to say
Well done.

Other times they yell, while gripping my hand with such force
that my blood starts thrumming and they sear me through
with wild
unseeing
eyes
and they beg me:

Let me go.

Like I am some kind of gatekeeper, like I can open a curtain,
or a window,
like the old Irish nurses used to do,
to let the soul escape.

Let me go!
Let me go!

they plead,
and I find their sight and hold their gaze,
and say:
It's ok, you can go now, you can go.
But still they cry

Let me go.
Let me go.

The hardest and the best are, of course, the parishioners who have become your friends – the ones you love and who love you too (which is against the Ministers Code of Ethics, not the love part but the friendship part, but we all do it, and cannot help it, and we kind of don't care what the rules say)

With my friend Margaret,
I visit every few days and I watch her journey from the land of the living
to the shadow place
of the now,
but not yet –
and then,
finally
she is gone.

This is what I see:

This visit, we drink tea and we talk about your funeral, you have it all prepared,
the hymns carefully chosen, you tell me what you want and I promise you I will make it happen. You look me clear in the eyes and I begin to cry.
You squeeze my hand.
Who is ministering to whom?

Remember when I was about to give birth to Nushy?
I say,
Remember how you knew that something was wrong?
Remember how you rang?

This next visit, the teacup is next to you, by the bed. It's like a little fist,
of polite resistance, held up, in the face of the grim reaper,
the one who's been biding his time, hanging out in the doorway.

Not yet.
The cup seems to be saying.
Not yet.
Next visit – no cup, just you.
Mouth
open.
Your teeth are out.
Your mouth too dry to put them in and what's the point anyway.
Your nighty is flannel and faded,
but it smells like lavender, like all old ladies' nighties. And it has been
ironed, even now.

It is almost Ascension Day
The day that story tells us Jesus rises up, up, up, up, up, up.
In the old paintings, you can sometimes see his toes, dangling, at the top.

Do you remember?
I say.
How we used to laugh
at this day
and now
your soul

*is floating
away.
You are going up too.*
I say.

We both want this,
to be true.

One visit with Margaret, we gather all the grown family around and she is wheeled into the lounge room. We are going to do an anointing, with olive oil from the kitchen, mixed with lavender from the bathroom. The grown daughters are giggling as they mix it up in a bowl.
We are going to baste you, Mum,
one calls, merrily, from the sink. Nothing could be more everyday than this.

The pouring of the oil
the gold of crushed olives
flowing into the Formica bowl,
the bowl that had been part of their childhood
the one that their mum whipped the butter in,
for every birthday
of their growing
and now they make fragrant oil,
(just like folk did back in Jesus' day)
to anoint the body,
the body that birthed them and held them and kept them warm with its weight,
now they say:

Thank you.
to that body,
with their own hands.

When we finally all gather around, some perching on the backs of chair, others at their mother's feet, the air grows thick with grief. I watch them. They are entering the ocean and they don't know if they can swim.

So, as always, I begin to speak, words will be our shelter and our boat. Words will carry us across the sea.

Jesus of the Sorrows.
who knows the solitary space of loss,
be our companion as we gather in our heartbreak.
Breathe your gentle presence into us.
Lover of all, who watches through the night, draw close to Margaret
and to we who mourn.
Calm our fear of abandonment.
Let us hold faith with one another that love reaches beyond death.
God who weeps, comfort Margaret
who is dying
May she die without fear.
God who in Jesus, stills the storm and soothes the frantic heart;
And carry Margaret in your arms as she departs,
rock her now,
be her boat,
carry her safe over this sea of grief.

Margaret, I anoint you now with the sign of the cross,
remember in this moment that you are a child of God,

beloved and precious in God's eyes.
And remember too, that though you walk in the valley of the shadow,
You do not walk alone.
And that God is with you.
To carry you home.

(Starting at the ankles or feet, over the blanket or on skin
Touch and encourage her family to touch.)

We commend and give thanks for these feet,
The journey that they have taken,
The body which they have carried,
The places they have been.
We place Margaret's feet at the feet of Christ.
(Move toward her hands or wrists)

And so it goes.

Gently, each part of the body is held and anointed and blessed. At one point, I catch the eye of the father, the husband – the soon-to-be widow. He is sitting back, watching his grown children weeping, with their mother. He seems becalmed.
Later, I ask him what he was feeling, and he responds:

I was thinking of all the milk.
Litres of it,
that her body made,
and that she fed them all with.
We should have bottled it, weighed it...

I was thinking about how,
you can't measure a life,
not really,
but that if you were to try,
all that milk,
feeding all those babies,
that would be a place to start.

the work 3

At careers days at high schools, no one says:

What about Ministry? You can visit the dying!
Do the rounds, like a district nurse but for the soul. You will drink lots of tea and sometimes the milk will be rancid. You will learn to drink black instant coffee. It is safer that way. You can unexpectedly find yourself being gripped by the hand of the man whom days before you had been playing chess with, who is now sweating and blind with fear, strapped to his bed and flailing, while the family looks at you, desperate:
say something, pray something,
make this better,
we are lost at sea, we are smashing,
on the rocks.

the work 4

Another funeral. No one I know. I get the call. Then they text me the details:
DOB, DOD, time of service, chapel, closest contact.
Then I make the call.
Mostly these calls are short, arranging to meet or talk again, sometimes the person breaks down, can't breathe, I sit in silence on the other end, waiting.

Standard funeral. A record needle in a groove, the service has clocked along, the stumbling eulogy by the nervous cousin, 'The Wind beneath my Wings' soaring beneath the slide show.
My face, straight.
It's time now to light a candle and place it in a bowl of sand.

Let this be a symbol of the light the person shone in your life and the life of the world.

My job in this moment is to keep rearranging the candles so the flames don't intermingle and cause a melting, tiny fire. I do this efficiently and invisibly, so no one feels their candle and its subsequent prayer has been misplaced or shuffled to the back of the bowl.
My job is to, discreetly, hold the shaking, elderly hands as they struggle to put the candle in the bowl, my job is to stop small children from getting burnt.

Two grown grandchildren come forward to light a candle,
before them, the multitudes of other funeral goers,
heaved into best polyester dresses, gold chains from anniversary birthdays
scooped around ageing necks.
Some are Catholic – they kiss the coffin.
The Irish – they grip the sides.
But these two, the grown-up grandchildren, stand before me,
and are pretending to be adults.
Until,
she goes to take the taper, and place it in the sand and he flicks it
out of her hands.
You bastard
she spits under her breath,
delighted.
And he
smirks
and life
stands up next to their grandmother's coffin –
and applauds.

the hit and run 2

Brian: Is Jayne there?

Ali: *No, no she's not here; I think she was staying at Craig's house. Is everything all right?.*

Brian: No Ali, no, this is Brian, everything is not all right. Brian, Craig's dad, everything is not all right. Craig has been killed, love.

It's my second year at drama school. I am 20.
The phone has just rung and I have just run
down the darkened corridor and now
we are here.

Here – in the streetlight-stained suburban midnight street.
You are all standing on the curb.
You are wrapped in doonas.
The police haven't left yet.
Lights flashing.
Red, blue, red, blue.
Like a heartbeat.
A policeman comes towards us, he looks about my age, he is, a boy.
**We are sorry to ask, but we need someone to come.
to identify
the body.**
My boyfriend gets into the back of the police car.

65

(He will be the man now.)
He will do this work.
We sit together on the black gash of the curb.
(We can't go back into the house.)
'He' is not there.
Later I ask:
What did he look like?
And you, dropped back by the squad car.
You say:
Tall.
He looked
tall
tall and skinny already.
His mouth was open.
He looked –
shocked. Dead shock.

I sometimes wonder,
if this was the moment when it became impossible to keep pretending
that everything was ok and that we were safe and that nothing bad was ever going to happen. Because of course –
in the blink of an eye,
the turn of the wheel,
the walk home in the dark, in the park,
the narrow wire look, in his eye,
the fast-growing mass,
the red light, that you missed,
the backing out in the driveway,
the screech of the brakes,
the quiet ultrasound,

the doctor clearing her throat,
the rain that won't stop falling,
just like that...
Nothing will ever be the same again.

So best grab it by the throat – all that darkness – grab it hard
and hold it close and
tear it apart
with your beak.
No more hiding, no more making nice.
All the cards are on the table, the gloves are off, the masks removed.
And I say:
I see you
face to face,
Death. So why don't you sit down and have a cup of tea?
Was this the moment
when I said yes to God?
Maybe.

the world 4

I love a platitude, don't you?
Especially straight after a funeral. Or in a hospital waiting room.
You know,
all those awesome things that people say
when they don't know
what to say.
Like:
It was probably for the best.
She's in a better place.
God doesn't give you more pain than you can handle.
He's gone to be one of Jesus' little angels.
that kind of thing...

Crow swoops down
and rips out
their eyes. I smile,
now is not the time to preach.

the pastoral visit 2

They say:
Blessed are they who mourn
but it can be hard to understand what on earth this means,
when you are falling deep down in the dark
or when you are sitting on the couch of a couple
who have lost their baby
and who fold and unfold
the tiny clothes in unsleeping hands.
I am sitting on this couch.
I arrived here this morning after receiving a phone call:

**You might not remember us, you married us... and our baby, our baby
has died.**

I pull the car up out the front of the suburban house,
and I know it is the right one,
because there is a change table out on the curb,
begging to be taken away.
I enter and sit down and when the television is muted,
we begin. To sit on the couch.
To have the conversation that no one ever imagines they will
ever have to have.

Do they make coffins that small?

the gravedigger 3

Tell us another story.
Um, well, there was this other time,
I was working with a new funeral director, you know,
and I think maybe it was her first time and we were in the chapel,
at the crematorium
and I'm down the front, I'm standing with the coffin,
and she, the funeral director, was sitting up the back,
getting ready to punch the button,
you know,
so that the curtains will open
and the coffin will sort of disappear on that rotating floor,
you know,
it's kind of like a Lazy Susan at a restaurant?
Oh yeah.
Anyway,
she pressed the button before I had finished,
and the floor started moving
and you and I
both know,
that there is no fire behind the curtain
but I reckon,
most people think the coffin goes straight into the flames,
and so I could see all these people's faces
they were watching me and watching the coffin,
and I knew they thought I was about to disappear,
into the furnace
and so they were kind of

*freaking out
but I hadn't finished the final prayer,
and so I had to kind of
race thru it
and then leap off,
at the last minute
before the coffin vanished.*
Awesome.
Yeah.

the world 5

I met a nun the other day and I found
her mere existence
deeply comforting...
Which was nothing to do with her
personally,
but more to do with that which Thomas Merton would call the
'this-ness'
of her.
And I wonder, if that's how people feel about the whole church
(at least those who do not actively hate it)
never attending – not even once – darkening the door,
but comforted,
at some unexamined level
to know that, somewhere there is a group of people,
getting together
to share stories of the unseen.
You are a minister!
people say to me
their faces alight with incredulity and wonder and, sometimes,
disgust.
A minister!
Like they have come across a unicorn
or a long-extinct,
half-forgotten, not very useful badger
just existing,
a revelation.

the world 6

**Good afternoon and welcome to Dying to Know day.
Today we will be learning about shrouds woven with mushroom spores ready to seed and the wild grave movement where paddocks are being bought to bury the bodies straight into the ground...
To kick us off we are going to hear now from Reverend Alexandra Sangster who works in the space of Death and Dying.
But before we begin, I'm curious ... Alex... Given the church's history as a brutal institution guilty of racism and sexism and homophobia and an image of god as intervening dictator, why would any rational person want to become a minister?**

Sometimes I'm asked to represent 'My Faith' or 'The Church' at events. Today it's at a conference for funeral directors. A whole floor of a motel has been given over to coffin displays, memorial YouTube sites and shrouds made of linen and mushrooms. You can even get show bags filled with helpful pens and small examples of marble, in different shades, for headstones. Today I am here to talk about grief. I say:

*The bereaved can be embarrassing.
We don't quite know what to do with them, or what to say.
A friend of mine, who was widowed young, said:*

People cross the street to avoid talking to me, I see them.

They look at their phones or pretend to be on a call.
They look up and down and everywhere – but at me.
Sometimes, in the early days of losing him, I felt like I should apologise,
like my pain was,
too much.
I'm sorry.
(I wanted to say)
I think my heart might be broken.
This is awkward.

I look out at the assembled group of funeral directors. They are the death walkers.
They do this stuff, every day. I tell them:

Steven Jenkinson, who worked for years in palliative care, once said something like:
Nobody gets to go to grief school. Grief is not a feeling, feelings are like weather:
they are not the architecture, they come and go, even the deepest feelings are transient.
But grief stays – grief is architecture, it carves you out from the inside.

I tell them how:

Our cultural death phobia means that many people feel they must grieve all alone rather than sharing the stories of the one that they have loved and lost and incorporating them
(incorporate from the late 14 century to bring back into the body,
from corporate,
to blend; to absorb, to eat)

not just into their own bodies but into the body of community.
We need to re-member (put the pieces of the body back together again)
and that way we can co-create wholeness,
(whole, holy)
whereas before,
there was only,
brokenness
and a terrible,
alienating,
loneliness.

I tell them:
A boy at my daughter's school has just died.
And the family have welcomed the community
the whole school,
to come to the funeral.
There will be a Rosary said,
and a High Mass held,
and then they will walk,
altogether, behind the hearse
towards the sea.
Un-measurable grief.

I then say:
Pay attention to how happy you felt, knowing that he will be farewelled, magnificently.
Pay attention to the ancestors inside you –
(the ones who shift in your bones and mutter into your mind)
Yes.
They are saying.
Yes, that's right. That is how

**it should
be done.**

Then I tell them:
*When I hear from folk that someone that they love has died, I ask:
When is the funeral?
And so often now, they respond:*
**Oh, no,
We are not having one.
He didn't want one.**
or
We decided not to... We might just get everyone together some time down the track, send him off, you know, with a few drinks.

I lean forward into the microphone.

There is a politics behind the privatisation of dying, by which I mean, that our capitalist culture declares that dying is an individual act that we must go through on our own and that grieving people must get on with grieving as effectively as they can so that they can resume their position in being productive in the capitalist system. Evidence of this can be seen in how most of us no longer wear special clothes that mark as out as grieving people, we no longer engage in communal rituals to hold us, as we mourn, and at a more structural level, for many people, within their work contracts there is the bare minimum of time allowed off from work to grieve.

I can feel the directors shifting uncomfortably in their chairs. This political talk is unexpected and unwelcome. The Funeral Industry loves capitalism.
It's all about the upsell.

Some things cannot be fixed.
They can only be held.
But they can make us bigger and more porous and more able to be
a bridge
for others to walk upon
when they are all alone
on the other side of the chasm,
that is death.

Later after the talk, I meet with the other speaker. She is a Death Doula and she is all floating cloth and strands of beads, she speaks with emphasis on odd words and is passionate about her work. I like her immensely. She tells me how:

Death Doulas help with the birthing of the soul but of course, I don't always tell the dying person that this is what is happening, because they don't always believe in the soul.

I imagine the soul of the person, slipping out a side door, the Doula leading the way with her fingers to her lips.

Shhhh, this way, off you go, nicely done, thanks for coming...
and all the while, the family sits, holding the hand of the empty body, weeping.

I think of all the times I have sat with people as they die and of how,
there is a moment,
when the soul leaves the body,
where the body sort of sinks

and then is emptied out,
like a tide,
receding
and of how the body then becomes,
what it has been all along,
a humble
empty
vessel.

It is always very quiet. When the soul goes.

I remember how, after my mother died; I couldn't bare to turn off the oxygen that had kept her alive for so long. It was such a comforting, rhythmic sound. It had been her companion, like a small wheezing dog, that had followed her from room to room and now it was, weirdly, the last of her. So, I couldn't pull
the switch.
I remember how her soul sort of hovered, mist-like, above her, bird-thin bones,
and of how we opened the window and of how
she
dissolved.

The Death Doula says:

Sometimes we are called Death Midwives, but I prefer Doula, it's more inclusive. What we do has been around forever and it is usually the women who do the work. Death shouldn't be

isolating or overly medicalised and we don't need to be afraid of it. Our job is to educate, support, inform and also, to just hold people's hands.
It's so messed up, what's happened to death, and people are so lonely.

She looks me in the eye.

It's good you're here, in the world. There's not many of us. Keep going. We stand at the crossroads, you and me, where everything is stripped away. It matters.

I feel strangely buoyed by her practical straight talk. She reminds me of my gran and I kind of want her to take me home. The organisers come over and I am thanked for giving my 'talk'. I am given a showbag and then I catch the lift down to the lobby where rich people wearing active gear have no idea that coffins are hovering over their heads. Which is metaphor enough for any Saturday morning.

the gravedigger 4

So, have you ever felt, like, spirits?
Yeah.
**Yeah, me too, I mean I see stuff and I feel it, sometimes.
Not scary, mostly, just there, you know.**
Yeah, I know.
What about evil?
What about it?
Well, do you believe in it?
*Um, well yeah, I suppose, I mean it exists doesn't it. The
big question is, where does it come from?*
So, what do you reckon?
*Well, I think that, maybe, evil is like a spiritual force,
And that sometimes – if we are super vulnerable, kind of
smashed up, by life,
it can find its way in.*
That doesn't seem fair.
No.

We both stand.
Quiet.
By the grave.

Then I say to him:
*I stopped a fight the other day. Between two street men.
One huge, like a barrel and young,
the other tall,*

80

the gravedigger 4

tall as a light pole
all bare
jutting cheek bones
and whipping,
winter coat.
The younger one was bawling, totally losing it.
Like in my face.
He was going:
Why does he even come here, he has a house, he has a family!
well
I said to him
He comes here because,
he is lonely,
just like you.

I was standing in the middle, between them both.
And then I looked up and they were both,
so big,
and I said to them:
Gosh, you are both, very, tall.
And they, shocked, looked down at me,
and across
at each other,
and then we all,
began to laugh.
and the possibility of violence,
slunk away...

Which is not a story of evil,
but maybe
of how,

it sometimes,
begins.

Later, thinking about it more, I remember how Jesus once said:
that evil is a legion and that it can invade,
and it can devour and destroy,
and so, we have to name it,
and call it out,
Whenever we can.

(Think little girl,
thrown off the Westgate bridge,
her brother telling his father:
she can't swim, daddy, she can't swim.
Think bodies in trucks,
and bodies in fields,
and my friend's grandma,
who kept herself alive in the Holocaust,
by playing the violin,
to the Nazis.
Think the little boy who was adopted and then given back,
think stolen children,
think sorry camp,
think gunman in the school,
think 5-year-old being taught how to 'shelter in place'.
Think
convent and teenage mother and buried baby and
think, think, think............ stop.)

Do not be afraid.

But mark this: those of us who can, need to step up
and hold
the
line.

the work 5

I was having a chat with a new friend the other day. This new friend is one of the recently released refugees from the Park Prison Hotel where my government had kept them, imprisoned in for over a year. Prior to this, the government had kept them on an island, some for as many as nine or ten years, an island covered
in stones.

We were meeting up for coffee; he bought me baklava and wanted me to go for a ride on his motorbike which I said no to because I'm a bit scared of motorbikes,
and he was telling me,
about the community order
that he has been released on
part of this community order means that he is not allowed to work,
so he's been doing volunteer work around the place,
helping people with gardens.
I used to work with big machines
he tells me.
From when I was a very small boy in Iraq,
all of the big machines
I have been a miner; I have done many things,
but now I volunteer.
He also told me that another restraint of the community order is that he must be home every night by nine o'clock,
and it explicitly states that he's not allowed to sleep outdoors.
I found this requirement astonishing and like something from a Kafka novel.

Why are you not allowed to sleep outdoors?
**I have no idea – but like a child,
I must be tucked up in bed by nine o'clock, each night.**
Later, after the coffee cups have emptied, I say:
How did you manage, how did you manage to stay sane?
He smiles.
**Many things.
I would walk 7000 steps back and forwards,
back and forwards,
in the motel room – everyday – I would count them.
Music – music helped – and all of you, standing outside the window,
knowing that we were not forgotten.
I learnt a long time ago to be patient and to not lose hope.**
This man's English is very good,
but I wasn't sure if he knew the root of the word patient.
Patient from the Latin, 12th century: quality being willing to bear adversities, calm endurance misfortune, from the Old French
pacience meaning suffering.
So, to be the patient is to be the one who suffers – which is why we send our patients to hospital.
I told him all this and he nodded.
**Yes
Yes
to be the patient is to be the one who is suffering. But you know, when I looked out the window, even though they covered them in black plastic, I could still,
just,
see
the
sky.**

the work 6

The coffin has been secured and I am standing in front of the hearse,
as it prepares to pull out
from the kerb
and enter the traffic.
I turn to give the driver 'the nod' to indicate that we can head off,
when I feel
someone's hand
in mine.
The hand belongs to the friend of the dead woman,
a tall man,
dressed like some latter-day Oscar Wilde,
and he staggers with the grief and with the booze,
and the uneven,
broken
bluestones.
Come on, Rev,
he says,
as he shifts his shoulders back
and then I realise that they have all come to join me
on the road.
All God's beggars.
With canes and bleary eyes and toothless mutterings these rough sleepers
and street folk
have come to walk their old friend,

down to the corner
and to say
a final
goodbye.
My Alb is flapping in the wind as I attempt to corral this crew
away
from stepping directly
in front
of the moving cars.
It's midafternoon and the road is humming.
Like a medieval mystery play we stop the traffic with our procession.
Their faces are set with seriousness.
They have carried the coffin and now they will walk her off.
This woman who lived alone and died alone in public housing,
who spent her days stealing fags
and getting in fights,
whose one room was filled
with plastic bags
full of plastic crap
and who died
with a tattered Bible
in her bed
is now being farewelled,
like a queen.

the world 7

I am picking up my girls from school.
I am standing alone at the monkey bars.
I am always alone at the monkey bars.
Word has got around...
She's a minister.
What – like in parliament? That's cool.
No like in the church –
Seriously?
Yeah, I know, right!

the call 2

run run run

So, I'm 23 now,
and I've done the whole actor thing.
(3 years at drama school, happiest I have ever been, minor roles on the telly, making my gran proud, playing prostitutes and street kids and staying thin forever)
and now I'm seeing angels in the architecture and crosses on the kitchen cupboards
and this idea:

(Minister, Minister, Minister)

just won't leave me alone.
My mother mutters about schizophrenia
and even I,
in my electrified state
wonder if, perhaps,
I am going
mad.
My new boyfriend is anxious,
This whole Christian thing, you're serious about it, yeah?
Yeah.
I confess, awkwardly.
Yeah.
Run run run.

Run run run.
I read a book about Breathwork, about how breathing can explode you out of your body and connect you into God. My mother knows a man who practises this work, an old Methodist minister man. I go to see him. Tell him all my dead friend stories and then say:
I want to find God.

Mmm, hmmm.
he nods.
I breathe with him for a year, week in week out, on a mattress, eyes closed, weeping, spinning, into space. I become: widow and orphan and cracked earth and ocean and then, shockingly, Christ –
crucified.
I sit bolt upright, arms outstretched:
Oh God, oh God... No! No! Anything but that!
The old man pushes me back down.
Breathe into it.
he says;
Breathe.

I go to a church.
I think I'm meant to be a Minister.
Mmmm hmmm
I'm not baptised, I don't get the whole Jesus thing – but I think this what I'm meant to do.
Mmmmm hmmmm, well you might want to start by coming to church?
Oh, um, yeah – Nah. Ok, I s'pose – but if it's really boring, I'm not coming back.

the work 7

We are sitting out the front of the church. She has left quickly,
in distress,
so I follow.

How do you feel?
I feel sad.
Yep.

We are sitting on the old wooden seat which leans against the red brick wall, the service has just finished, and I am still vibrating, with all the words and all the spirit, that have coursed through me.

(Sometimes,
after I have finished leading a service,
I feel like a sailing ship,
becalmed,
all the wind
spirit, pneuma,
dissipated and my body –
rocking.)

This woman has intelligent eyes, clouded by medication and by fear.
Her speech pattern is hesitant, chasm-filled,
she could slip off at any moment

and go into
freefall,
plummeting down the gaps.
I have to go... slow.

Did you feel sad before you came?
Yes
Yes. There's lots to be sad about isn't there?
Your mum is gone, my mum is gone, those men in there have lost their whole families.
Mary lost her son and the war in Ukraine.
Yes
Sometimes it's good to be sad with other people.
Not to be sad all on our own.
Yes

It's Easter Sunday. The first one for me at this new ministry placement and I had been dreading it. (We don't have 'jobs' in the church – we are 'called' to a 'Placement' and then we are 'Placed'... like God has picked us up and plonked us down).
I had been dreading it because they are always a big deal, these High Holy days.
Filled with expectation – a big sermon, a big crowd, big music.
But here,
in this ragtag church,
with its tiny congregation and its rough sleepers outside,
this church,
sitting on the filthy, rubbish blown, empty street,
I was sure that no one would come.
I was wrong.
Through the rectangle of light that is the door, step the men.

Refugees.
Just released only 10 days ago from the Park Prison Hotel,
and with them
come a small group of women, they have been the witnesses.
(During the year of the refugee's incarceration, activists sat and sang and rallied outside the motel until the men were eventually set free.)
And here we all are, together.
I was not expecting the refugees to arrive this morning; most of them are Muslim and all of them are in shock, yet here they are on Easter Day, sitting in my church,
and weeping.

The Easter story –
of wrongful imprisonment
and invasion
and escape
and families ripped apart,
and the breaking
of hearts,
has never seemed so relevant,
or devastating
as it does today.
(Son, this is your mother; Mother, this is your son.)
Later, after my sad woman on the bench has left,
I am standing under the bright blue sky with one of the men.
I can't get enough of the sky
he tells me,
I must be outside now, all the time.
and he shows me a photo on his phone,
of his

Do they make coffins that small?

beautiful boy
that he has never met,
cheeky as they come, eyes bright,
like an otter pup.
We laugh together at this little boy's shiny funny face.

A tiny rising (he is risen, risen indeed)
amongst the pigeons and the wind,
in a scruffy garden
on Easter Day.

the work 8

Will you look after my things?
Yes
All my things, my papers, my writing, just in case, you know any of them come looking... one day... I mean, they probably won't...
but if they did...
When I left home,
when I was a lad
my mother,
she shoved a pound note in my hand
it was all she had.
I can't tell anyone that story, you know
and all the stories...
Maybe I should burn it, all of it, in boxes.
No one is ever going to come looking. But maybe the little one, maybe Daisy,
she might want to know about her grandpa, none of the others, of course, I remind them of their mother, my daughter, God she was bright, did I ever tell you about her, before the drugs, before they took her kiddies away, God she was the smartest of the lot...
Maybe Daisy will come looking...
I just want to know that they will be safe...
will you take them?
Yes.
People give me (well they give the church)
things to hold on to.

Do they make coffins that small?

I climb up the ladder that flings down from the ceiling and I heave the boxes
up to the top. There is an attic up here and in it is:

2 cardboard angels,
3 boxes of decaying Christmas decorations,
1 folded pile of costumes for small wise people, an evil king, soldiers, a sheep, Mary (blue tea towel) and at least three mangers.
1 horror movie plastic baby doll Jesus.
20 pairs of respectable women's shoes from over 50 years ago, from the days when the church had a choir and the choir master demanded that the women wear black shoes and would get cross if they didn't, so they decided to keep pairs at the church – to keep him placated
but then, when the choir folded
(all those thin sopranos, quavering, in the pews)
no one threw them away
and all the women died
but their shoes are still here,
waiting for rehearsal to begin.
10 boxes filled with the minutes from a million meetings going back for 50 years or so.
Also, one box filled with the diaries of a 17-year-old girl
who fled her father but wanted to store her childhood
(old paints, photos of a grandma, teenage novels, school reports).
I helped her bring them here, after the court case, where I had been her witness and she asked for a restraining order, against her father,
which was granted,

by a female magistrate, who looked
the trembling girl
in the eye
and said
Well done, well done.
And finally, five boxes filled with the remains of a marriage
(the camping gear, the broken lamp, the old toys, the painting
she never liked anyway)
all spilling out of hastily packed crates.
If I am very still,
I can hear them:

Get out get out.
Jesus, woman, I'm going, give us a break, calm down. I'm going.
NOW! Right now! And don't you try and keep those keys, put them down, down on the table!

In the attic, I also find other lives stored away, given to other ministers, from other days.
People think that the church will be here forever.
But I watch the moon
rise and
fall
upon the straits of the cloud-tossed sky
and I know
it won't.

Recently, the grown-up children of ministers who have died
give me their fathers'
(for it is always fathers)

old travelling communion cups.
This is for you,
they say,
and I am deeply moved and grateful, but also know that I will never be able to fill
all these cups
with the symbolic blood,
of the weeping Christ,
even if I did communion for days on end.
Their cups,
runneth over
and I am left holding the chalice,
that no one ever wants to drink from anymore.
Take
I say to the empty church,
this is my blood, poured out for you.

Sometimes being a minister feels like being the caretaker, at the end of time.
I stand in the sanctuary (the bit up where the altar sits, where you can't be arrested in medieval times) contemplating this building full of memory and prayer
(and burnt-out husks of candles and hymn books soft with singing).
I wonder what I should do, with all these boxes.

Will you look after my things?
Yes, I will... for as long as I can...

the call 3

So, in the church you don't just rock up for an interview, you are 'called' and you 'respond to the call' and part of the response, sometimes, involves running away. Because, let's face it, no one wants to be a minister.

Run, Run, Run!
fast forward through this bit, it takes a couple of years...
Run
away
and pretend that everything will be
Ok
but you know it's not.
Run, Run, Run!
Like an Escher painting –
up and down the stairs
always ending up in the same place.
What's it all about, sweetheart?
Do you want to save the world?
Who do you think you are?
Can't you just be a social worker?
Is it because all those people died?
When you were growing up?
Is that what this is all about?
Maybe you should make a list... ?

the list

Age 2:
Old Age – My poppy, the first death, someone is burning all the books outside his house, they are carrying out boxes filled with his belongings and burning them.
My mother puts her hands into the flames, she rakes thru ashes:
No, no, this is his life!
she cries.
What are you doing!

Age 9:
Car accident – Cassie, neck snapped, death by drowning in the Yarra,
her little boy is three,
Look after Edward
they say,
**the police are here,
look after him.**
Hey Edward, do you want to play?
Mummy, where is my mummy?

Age 11:
Asthma Attack – Mathew, blond, Botticelli angel
we played in the dam,
do you remember? We were all together and we kept falling in.
Do you remember?

You wore a gypsy scarf and painted cheeks, lips like cherries.
You can't breathe!
Why can't you breathe?
Breathe!
You were dead at 17.

Age 13:
Death by suicide. Johnny. Hose in car.
His blue, stupid, beautiful,
blue
eyes.

Age 19:
Old Age – The usual – Nana

Age: 20:
Suicide – Another cousin, another car

Age 21:
Hit and Run.
Craig, sitting on your bike. the car striking you, from behind.

Age 22:
Suicide – My sister's friend – jumped off the Westgate.
Her mother should have fixed her jaw
our mother said.

I dream of Craig – all the time:
Your mouth is open

Do they make coffins that small?

I wake up to tell you,
I had the most terrible dream.
I dreamt you died and died and died and died and you wouldn't stop.
But you are not here.
It was not a dream...

So, there is the list.
Everyone has one.
This is mine.

the work 9

You!
She spits at me from her widow clothes, all black and torn and crumpled cloth.
You, who are you?
You homeless?

She is sitting, muttering on the bench out the front of the church. She is surrounded by the men, the ones who are always there,
smoking a joint and passing the time,
come rain or shine.
The men greet me with gap-toothed smiles, baseball caps on backwards and tattoos,
all faded on their faces.

Hey

they say, they are happy to see me.
But this woman...
You!
You, who are you?
You homeless?
No
I respond,
No, I mean I could be, but I'm not.
I'm the minister.
Minister! Hah, you are not, you look like teenager, your hair, it is mess, and you in jeans, you homeless!

I brave her scorn and sit next to her on the bench, and she continues to belittle me for my fashion. It is International Women's Day and the irony that I am being berated on a bench by an angry bag lady is not lost on me. Finally, I open the church, go in and get my Alb and stole, and I put them on in front of her
Ta da!
I say,
Told you so!
I say.
Finally, she smiles.
Yes, yes, now you are priest.
You should wear that –
all day, all the time and then we will know who you are.

the call 4

Run, Run, Run!
Hang out at the high rise with kids whose lives are bleak with broken promises.
Run!
Sing songs with refugee women who have carried their whole lives in their hands.
Run!
Then
finally
fall
down upon my knees on the asphalt of Sydney's Surrey Hills
down and weeping
I give in!
(Shouting to the sky)
I give in!
(Foolish now, you must look ridiculous, what are you doing, get up).
Weeping.
What do you want me to do?
What do you want me to do?
Blue sky, empty now.
Minister.

the work 10

Pedofile.

The church door has been graffitied again.
Bright, red, smeared, and misspelt and the message couldn't be clearer.
Whoever wrote this, in the night, has been
very,
very,
broken
and has written in red, all over both the church doors. It looks like blood.
(*Take drink, this is my...*)
I roll up my sleeves and start scrubbing. Tea tree oil is best for this, the astringent cuts through.

Beware. Protect your children.

I am wearing my clerical collar and I am scrubbing the door and a woman walking past pushing a pram, calls me over. Her baby smiles up at me and the mother asks for directions. My hands are wet and red, and I wipe my hair from my face and I watch her gaze travel from me to the door I have come from and then I see her, see, the word.

Pedofile.

(Oh God, not me, I'm not the pedophile, please don't think it's me).
I see from the outside,
this image:
The mother and child.
The minister.
The words in red.
(I am falling to my knees, I am so, so, so, so, sorry for what the church has enabled,
perpetrated
and destroyed).
I return to my work.
Penance of the Ages.
I will need to buy more tea tree; this bottle is empty and this work –
is not going to be finished,
any time
soon.

the work 11

The old man is stumbling, the wind icy, he is pressed into the brick of the alley.

This is one of my parishioners, one who was once
a pillar,
a rock,
a cornerstone of the church.

Interesting – our highest praise for someone is that they are:
solid
of the earth,
hewn from mountain.
It is like we know, instinctually, from deep time, inside ourselves, that rocks are holy, full of power. And how we know that first peoples recognise some rocks as sentient and full of agency. And how we know that in the old stories, from the Bible, the Rock is another name,
for God:

'Do not tremble and do not be afraid;
Have I not long since announced it to you and declared it?
And you are My witnesses.
Is there any God besides Me,
Or is there any other Rock?
I know of none.' (Isaiah 44:8)

And that Jesus spoke of how if justice is not done then:

The very stones will cry out.
We know all this.

Which is why, perhaps, that we have walked to them and around them and have carried them and why kings still sit upon them and why we pray to them and call them, in Australia, the heart, of our country.
And why this old man, was known as one, until he began,
to fall.
This man, clouded by dementia...
plummeting,
earthbound.

Arthur? Arthur? Are you ok?

I catch up with him,
shelter with my body,
he looks up,
up
to my great height
from his
diminishment,
he is self-descending,
back to bone.
Were you always such a tiny man?

Arthur? Arthur? Are you ok?

The clearing of the eyes –
the temple of the curtain is torn in two,

he
sees
me
He begins to speak, the bewilderment
(be wild, lost in desert, wind whips, tear your clothes,
howl
into the indigo
ink, black sky)
in his voice,
catches my heart.
(Like when a child catches your hand and begs you not to leave.)

I am losing, I am losing, I am losing my capacity.
Oh Arthur.

(Voice through me, not me)
I am,
crow
(black feathers unfurl from fingertips,
backbone fills with air,
no mucking about now)

Oh Arthur, you have done so well,
faithful servant, and with you
God is so pleased.

He hears me – he understands – eyes fill with tears.
Arthur! Arthur!
It's Winsome, his wife of 60 years.

Arthur, what's wrong?
Bustling towards us, the curtain falls, the moment passes.

Crow shakes feathers,
and hops off,
into the
ice
light.

We are all humans together again, in the carpark and its bloody freezing out here.

We're all right, Winsome; we are all right.

the call 5

Dear Alexandra, we are pleased to advise you that you have been accepted as a candidate to be trained as a Minister of the Word.

the word
in the beginning
in the beginning was the word
and crow realised that god spoke crow
just existing
was his revelation.
Standing on a cliff edge
ocean
dazzle
bright
white
light
shining
shot through and broken apart.
I am
splintered
into a 1000 pieces
I am
not
I
I will spend my days,
walking around
like
a lighthouse.

the work 12

She is dripping wet and covered in soap.
The shower is pelting down, and the floor is a flood.
Somehow, the two of us, have ended up, here.
In this bathroom. At the Drop In
And she is naked and wild and angry, and she has no teeth so I can't
understand what she's saying or even if she can understand me, but I have to get her out of here.
We are closing soon, and the other punters are getting anxious.
When she came in, an hour or so ago,
I didn't know if she was a man or a woman,
so thin was her form,
so baggy her clothes
and teeth... well, teeth have a way of shaping a face,
(which I have never thought about before, but it's true).
Teeth give us humanity,
and personality
and scaffolding.
They hold up our face, in a way, and when we have a face,
we can face the world.
She is yelling at me again, very close and very wet. This isn't going well.
We have to get you dry.
I say,
and she throws the towel, onto the lake-like floor.
Ok, Ok... how's about, um... Did you have a mum?

She shakes her head,
How about a grandma?
Again the emphatic dismissal, the groan of no.
Ok
I say.
Well maybe, once, a long, long time ago when you were little, maybe there was a woman who dried you? And maybe today, I could be that woman?
Would that be ok?
She nods and so I begin.
A rough dry-off really, her shoulders her legs,
She is laughing and wriggling. I see the small,
seal slip
of the child
she once was.
Dry enough, undies on, fresh clothes.
I get her out of the bathroom and sit with her at the table.
You have to go now.
I say.
I know, I know I have to go
she mutters,
I promise I will go if you let me sing to you.
Ok.
I say.
Ok.
We gather up her possessions –
the methadone, the fags and a torn children's picture book –
into a new hessian bag and head outside into the sun.
I kneel beside her, and she begins to sing,
about hearts breaking and love and the sky.
She is shy but happy as she sings,
and I am split in two,

with the whole goddam thing,
and then she staggers off,
into the streets.

the work 13

Spent the morning with a small group of high school kids
who are all in danger of dropping out.
Kids on the edge, kids on the margin,
kids in freefall with nowhere to land.
Except
maybe
here.
In this group, that I am visiting.
Where they catch each other.
One girl starts to tell a story about her childhood.
Not like what others have
she says, flinging out her pain like you would fling out a
'good morning'
or a casual 'g'day'.
Until she realises that people,
her classmates and the adults
are sitting soft,
and actually,
listening,
and so she slows down and her bravado falls away like mist
and then
there she is,
just her and her
terrible
pain.
The storytellers I am with
give her story back,

like a journey to grandma's house,
thru the dark,
wolf-ridden woods.
They talk about how,
sometimes,
it can take a really, really long time,
to get there.
When it's over, she nods, from beneath her beanie and her hood and her hair.
Yeah
she says.
That's it.

the world 8

Later, in the country town,
(where we have stopped for coffee to fuel the long drive home)
I go into the op shop to search for crockery,
(coz you can never have too many striped blue bowls).
Ohhh, this was Val's
says a woman dusting the shelves.
Aww and this too.
She is picking up the bric-a-brac and holding it up to the winter light.
Oh look – she loved this.
Val's china shepherdesses have ended up here, ready to be sold.
Put it down!
barks the other woman from behind the counter.
Leave it alone and come and help me sort these socks.
Suddenly, my friend,
who is tall and wearing a good winter coat,
and who has windswept hair,
down to his shoulders,
appears at the op shop door.
Oh lawd, look, now here's Jesus
says the woman, who has been holding her dead friend's china.
Just what we need
says the other.
Just what we need.

ghosts 2

The linen is wrapped around the body in clean, folded lines.
It looks like Furoshiki, the Japanese practice of wrapping objects.
Precious things.
But this,
is a body.
I think of other things tightly wrapped.
Like Christo and Jeanne Claude's bridge in Paris.
Like the tiny shells my oldest daughter would knot up, in scraps of fabric,
and hide away inside her undie's drawer.
Like the teeth of my girls,
which I could not bare to throw away
(all that milk)
so I wrapped them in my Grans hankies
and put them in my jewellery box.
Like a secret.

This body is in a shroud.

Shroud: the word comes from the Old English and means,
among other things:
a cloth, which envelops and conceals,
also
a winding-sheet,
for a dead body,

and
fantastically,
a strong rope, supporting the mast of a ship,
without the rope, the ship was said to be:
naked.
So, this shroud is concealing and supporting
this body,
for its last work. That of dissolving
into earth.

This body belonged to a woman who chose to end her life through Voluntary Assisted Dying. This woman, whose body I last saw, lying in a hired hospital bed,
in the middle of her lounge room,
with a plugged in cooling blanket,
resting gently on top,
is now,
gone.

Her earthly remains lie at my feet,
wrapped up and covered in wattle.
Wattle, according to the Yorta Yorta people, is the death flower.
My grandpa knew this. He told us:
Never have it in the house.
And so, we never did.

Wattle is also, our 'National' symbol, we gave it to our soldiers as they marched into the desolation of WW1 and when the

troops evacuated Gallipoli, an army chaplain, scattered silver wattle seed
(that he had soaked in water for 20 hours)
between the graves,
so that the dead soldiers,
were not
alone.

The woman who died was a climate activist and, at her funeral, some of her friends came dressed as endangered species. They sat up the back of the church.
A whole pew of them, staring at me, through their felted eyes.
They all looked, slightly accusing and very sad.
Which made sense.
At many levels.

And now we are here. By the grave, in the bush.
About to lower her wrapped up body, slowly, with ropes,
into the ground.

The cemetery where this burial is taking place is the same cemetery where most of my ancestors lie. It's where I came as a child to visit all the relatives and then eat boiled egg sandwiches, with my gran, by the graves.

My mum is here.

As I stand and hold space for this woman's farewell, I feel a hand, slip, into mine.

Ghost hand.
It is my great, great Aunty Elsie. The one who fell, fitting from the apple tree, when she was only 21. She is standing next to me
and she is happy that I am here.
The sun is pouring out over the mountain,
the crow's wheel overhead,
and the earth,
accepts her own.

the work 14

We have been drinking coffee, she has been telling me about
her boyfriend, about what she is studying and then there it is,
in between us, like liquid,
like an almost
palpable, invisible energy,
like I could touch it,
like I could tap it with my spoon and it would ring out
a clear high note.
So, I ask her.
Have you ever thought about becoming a minister?
She starts, pupils dilating, breath catches as a laugh and then
escapes, as tears, then more laughter.
Oh God, I mean, um, yes... yes, I think I do?
How did you know? I don't think I even knew.
Crow tilts his head, looks up from the table, upon which he
stands.
God
I say, with a wry smile.
God tells me stuff.

the work 15

Some churches are filled with light, pouring from windows stained with colour and some have granny rugs knitted by old ladies in bright discordant shades and some are like poverty theatre, stripped back to a stack of plastic chairs and a lopsided kitchen table.
Others take your breath,
and spiral it,
upwards
to the ship's-bow pitched ceilings and you find yourself wanting to lie on the floor and look
up,
up,
up.

But this one is dark,
really dark,
the wood,
the lighting,
the carpet and the people -
who are dressed in black.

Another funeral, this time I know the brother of the woman who has died. I married him 5 years before, he's a radical lefty who dumpster dives and who, every now and again, drops off bags of bread at my door, in the night.

It is this man's sister who is now to be buried.
She has taken her own life,

quietly,
zipped it up in a bag
and thrown it off a seaside cliff.
Her teenage daughter stands
mute,
by the coffin out the back. She will not leave its side.
So here we are.

The dark church is unfamiliar, I'm running around trying to work out where the matches are and checking microphones and power points, when I see her, the old crow woman, hunched in black, muttering, eyes wild, rosary clasped.
Is this your mother?
I ask the brother.
Yes
I go over, bend down, she looks up.
I am the priest.
I say, slowly.
She grabs out for my hand, and I can feel her bones, within a thin glove of skin.
She is strong, surprisingly strong.
This...
She spits.
This is a funeral?
Yes.
Whose funeral is this?
I swing around to catch the brother's eye. Now I see that all the gathered family is with him, a semicircle of agony, all looking at me.

Doesn't she know?

I ask, over my shoulder, my hand still gripped by hers.
No, well she has dementia, we didn't know how to do it, what to say, we were hoping, maybe... you could tell her.

Like a slow avalanche of large stones inside me, I am pulled down by their weight, I can feel my whole self, sliding, into the carpet, then deeper to the wood and then finally into the cold and hidden earth. On the outside, I am upright and they are all waiting. I look back at this ancient woman with her wild eyes, she too is beseeching.

Whose funeral is this?

The funeral is about to begin. The funeral director is waiting, ready to process the coffin.

Oh my love.
I say, still on my knees,
I am so sorry.
I speak very slowly. She is watching my mouth.
I am so sorry.
This is your daughter's funeral. This is Jenny's funeral,
Your daughter,
she has died.

She looks to her son for confirmation. Eyes back to me.
And then it begins.
The keening.

Oi, Toi Toi, Oi, Toi Toi, Ohhhhhh, Oi, Toi Toi

Her mouth a wound.
In the side of a mountain.
Primordial,
pouring forth.
We are drowning in her sound,
it rises like water and laps at our throats.
I remember the role of the chorus in early Greek theatre, how they would stand by the body and wail. I remember the Celtic keening women, the mnathan-tuirim,
who would bang on the coffin and chant, but she,
this mother,
she is all alone.

I remember the words of the Hebrew prophet Jeremiah when he said:

Now you, Woman, hear the words of God.
Teach your daughters how to wail,
teach one another to lament.
Death has climbed in
through our windows.

I unfurl her hands from mine.
Come here!
I hiss to her dumbstruck son,
Come here!
and he stumbles forward to take his mother
into his grown-up arms
I stand,

Do they make coffins that small?

unsteady,
stumble forward like a drunk,
and then righten myself
I am a ship that has almost tipped-
over.
I look to the funeral director,
and the coffin enters the church.

the work 16

It is 4 a.m. and I have just edged my way out backwards from an enormous truck. The sand shifts beneath my feet and the darkness of the desert sky pours into my body like indigo ink. It's cold, so cold in this Queensland outback that my teeth begin to chatter.

The truck that I have just got out of is a big one with a trailer and a built-in kitchen. Custom-built by a man called Stew, designed for rough-riding and bush-bashing and this morning it has been bumping down a dirt road for hours. There are 7 of us on this journey, some are Religious (with a capital R as in this is our vocation and others are Activists (with a capital A because this is what they have dedicated their lives to) and we are all going up to the gates of the Adani workers camp. A gate that we are about to block, to stop the workers from heading out to the yet-to-be-dug coal mine. We are here with the blessing of the Wangan and Jagalingou people who have been at the frontline of this rolling protest from the beginning. In their own words:

We DO NOT consent to the Carmichael mine on our ancestral lands.
We DO NOT accept Adani's 'offers' to sign away our land and our rights and interests in it. We will not take their 'shut up' money.
We will PROTECT and DEFEND our Country and our connection to it.

And they have called on people to come and help them in their defence of country.
And so, we have come. We gather up our bags and banners and I put on my Alb over my puffer jacket. We are super quiet as we move to the gates, me, two ordained Buddhists, a Quaker and some other Christians. We set up chairs, unfurl flags and wait. As the rising sun stains the ice-blue, morning sky with gold, we can see the workers, already driving towards the gates, they come to a rattling halt at the sight of the closed gates and the random clergy.

For f-&#'s sake!
spits one, getting out his ute and striding towards us,
What the hell, get out the bloody way or we'll call the cops!

Our spokesperson moves forward and tells the gathered men why we are here, he apologises for interrupting their workday, he talks about the climate and about catastrophic species loss, about children, and about the Great Barrier Reef.
The men swear again and one of them yells:
Smoko, boys!
And then they all get back into their utes and roar away.
We wait again and while we wait, we pray.

Prayer: The word comes from the 1300s and means
'earnest request, entreaty, petition' and also
'the practice of praying or of communing with God'.
In the history of Christianity there are really just two major ways of thinking about God and how God relates to the world. The first is 'supernatural theism' which imagines God,

as a person-like being
and tells the story of how,
a long time ago,
this person-like being created,
everything
and occasionally
would intervene in the world.
The second concept imagines God as the
encompassing spirit
in whom everything lives and moves and has its being.
This second concept replaces the notion of divine intervention,
with divine intention
and divine interaction,
and we become,
co-creators
with God,
filled with God's Spirit.
So, God
becomes the Sacred within the universe,
and the Christian story
is one way,
that this Sacred can be understood.
But it's not the only way.
And prayer is love in action,
love poured out from our bodies,
and our hearts,
and this love
joins with the beating love of our immanent god,
who we feel,
in earth,
ocean,
tree,

rock,
and in each other.
Pulsating.
Simple.
One of my Buddhist friends begins to chant.
Soft and low.
The sun is high in the sky now and I am stunned with grief.
So sorry so sorry.
I say to the soil.
I am utterly aware of the insignificance of this action.
There are ice-skating rinks inside supermarkets in Dubai, spewing forth air-conditioning into the desert. There are floating islands of plastic in the ocean. There was a pregnant sperm whale washed up dead, only last week, on an Italian beach and when they opened her up, to discover the cause of her dying, they found, not only her dead baby but nearly 50 pounds of plastic jammed into her belly. There is my own country Australia where the fires have ripped up the east and west coasts and koalas with burning paws are sitting, stunned in the black burnt sticks of their homes. There have been landslides and flooding and an old man standing on a chair in his hallway as the water surges around his neck. He is making a last phone call to his son when he hears the farmer from the neighbouring property paddle past in a canoe.

I'm in here, mate!
he yells.
I'm in here.

There have been two new parents trapped in flood mud as their baby lies just out of reach who are rescued by a woman on ropes who has seen the landslide from the valley and who had a feeling in her gut that she should go and check. This woman swings on her ropes, like an angel over mud, and scoops the baby, into her arms.

The climate catastrophe has begun. It is now.

I feel Country under my feet. Humming.
This action, this drop in a wave, is at least a drop and that's what waves are made of.
That's what I told my children before I left home a week ago. And now that I am here, I can actually believe my own words. This
matters.
A crow circles overhead and euphoria mixed with devastation fills my heart.
I feel Jesus standing next to me, smiling wryly.
Keep going. Keep going.

One of the creatures most threatened, locally, by this massive mine,
is the tiny,
black throated finch.
This mine,
will destroy,
the last major habitat of this soft brown and robin blue bird.
The finch has become,
an

endling
an animal that is,
the
last
of its kind.
We are the witnesses
to this great
unmaking.

(And once upon a time, in the beginning of the beginning, there was a smashing and clashing of stars and God said: Let there be light!
And there was light! And there were made all manner of creeping creatures and all the birds of the air and all the fish of the sea and all the creatures, teeming in the deep and then God clapped God's hands and God rejoiced).

On average, we are losing 383 species a day. 383 endlings.

How lonely it must be, to be the last your kind.
Calling in the night, to see if anyone will answer.
When I gave birth to my youngest daughter, after all the groaning and the heaving and the splitting in two, after everyone had gone and it was just her and me, I cradled her tiny face and sobbed and sobbed and sobbed.

You will be all alone.
I wept.

One day when we have died and your sisters have died and you are a very old lady,
you will be all alone,
the very last one.

My grief was ridiculous; it became, a self-mocking story to tell, but I can feel it now, and it still
stops
my breath.

Four hours later (this place is remote), the paddy wagon spins through the dust and the police get out and stride up.
Here we go again.
One mutters and I understand his frustration.
None of us wants to be here.
It's bloody hot now and the flies are straight from a particularly vindictive version of hell. We begin the theatre of protest. We tell them:

We believe,
that as people dedicated to the common good, inspired by our beliefs,
and energised by our spirituality,
people of all faiths can and should be at the forefront of creating a safe climate...
And so we are here, with the blessing of the Wangan and Jagalingou people,
to prayerfully and peacefully protest against this mine.

They try to reason with us, try to get us on side, they get angry, they pour scorn, they try whatever they can to get this over with, as quickly as possible. Finally, they read us our rights and arrest us. The policewoman who is given the task of restraining me, turns me round and then says:
Hah! I think I arrested you last time.
Oh yes, yes.
I say,
I think you did, how have you been?
I had a baby!
The words leap out of her, she can't help it. She is clearly very happy.
Oh my goodness
I say,
That's so lovely.
Look,
She pulls out her phone and we stand in the sun while she flicks through photos on the screen. Later, as we wait for another police car to come and pick us up to take us back for processing (fingerprints, photographs, locked in a cell), one of the constables opens his lunch box and offers me a Vegemite sandwich. They are cut into triangles, and he has a juice box as well which he must have put in the freezer overnight, to keep his sandwiches cool. He stretches his long legs as we sit in the shade of a lonely tree and tells me how, before he became a policeman, he had studied environmental science and how, he's
Against the mine, you see, but people need jobs and what can you do.
Crow lands at our feet and the policeman shares his crusts. The adrenaline of the early morning has seeped away and I am all becalmed in the heat.

Thank you, Country.
I whisper, as I close my eyes.
I will keep trying.

the gravedigger 5

Where to from here?
Going down to the crematorium.
What are ya doing there?
I'm going to watch my friend.
I'm going to watch my friend burn.
Yeah?
Yeah... I promised her I would.

Normally, the body goes to the crematorium alone, normally the family waves goodbye at the funeral home, after the minister and the funeral director bow in front of the hearse (memories of musical theatre choreography flashing through my mind) and then off they go. But when I talked to Margaret about what she wanted for her funeral, she asked me if I would go with her, on this final step.
I don't want to be alone, it's silly, I know.

This walking before a hearse bit. It matters. Sometimes, when I do this walking, everything, shimmers.
Once,
only once,
I did this walking, up a busy Melbourne street with trams and shops and noise and everything
stopped
and time
cascaded

concertina like into itself,
and the current age melted away and the tarmac dissolved,
and the buildings faded and then there was nothing but hot
dry bush and a gentle walking uphill, on Country. I felt deeply
shocked but very happy all at once and then, with a rush, it all
came back and I was on the concrete again and the cars were
waiting, impatiently, for death to pass.

I head down the back driveway entrance to the crematoria.
I enter the warehouse cavern,
where the coffin sits.
This is awkward.
These high-vis-wearing men don't normally have visitors.
They shuffle and cough.
One of them approaches.

You the minister?
Yep.
The men wanted to know if you wanted to do anything?
Do anything?
With the coffin, you know.
Oh yes, yes, I do.

I look to the men,
standing in this loading bay.
Their arms
crossed
the easy stance of men
at work,
waiting,

talking quietly, about the weekend, the footy, the wife.

I raise my hands.
I lift her spirit –
with my fingers –
just in case there is any of her
left
entwined
caught up in the ribcage,
beneath the body and the clothes.
I lie my face upon the wood
I whisper and I bless.
The high-vis men lower their voices,
and Crow
hops,
approvingly around

The foreman nods his question.
All good, love?
All good.
The coffin is wheeled away.
I go to the viewing room.
I try not to think of the holocaust.
There is a box of tissues placed discreetly and behind me in the
bright
sunshine the wheelie bins overflow with fresh flowers.
While they unload
and prepare for the burning
I distract myself with the flowers,
could I take some of the flowers?
On my way out?

I mean they are just being thrown away,
and they are so pretty.
But maybe someone will see me. Is it stealing to take the discarded lilies of the dead?
And, of course, there is always the chance that, maybe, I would bring back more
than
the iris
the rose
the marigold.
Maybe the wisps of the souls would come too?
I think about flowers and about laying them on graves. Apparently, this is something we have always done. Some of the earliest examples include burial caves in Northern Iraq where traces of pollen and flower fragments were uncovered in the soil of a burial site from 62,000 BC.

But not all burials involve flowers.
In Australia, Mungo Lady, whose 42,000-year-old remains were found in an ancient, dried-up, eleven-kilometre lake, up past Mildura in country New South Wales, was first cremated, then her bones were crushed,
then her bones were burnt again,
and then she was, finally,
buried
in the white sand dunes of the lake.

Dead, Dead, Dead.

No trace of pollen in her ash.

Mungo Lady was found with Mungo Man and her remains, her story and her burial site are all cared for by the Paakantji and Ngiyampaa and Mutthi Mutthi people. Mungo Lady is the oldest known cremation ever to be discovered and her burial reveals the early emergence of humanity's spiritual beliefs.
Her burial reveals –
love.
She and Mungo Man are particularly special to their Aboriginal descendants who still live around the Willandra Lakes area. The people are proud of what the ancient remains prove of their endurance in the land and their survival from the distant past. Many believe that Mungo Man and Mungo Lady returned to teach us (all of us) about what matters.

Spirit,
still here
fire,
bone into ash,
ash into earth,
(we are but dust and ashes)
spirit into place,
and you can feel the red earth,
breathing.

Once, while out in this desert, we took the kids, with a Discovery Ranger called Ernie,
out into the shining white lunar landscape of the sand dunes which surround the lake.
And while Ernie told the adult stories of deep time and burial, the children, ran.
Go for it, kids,

Ernie had said,
and like puppies, let off the leash, they were off.
Wild things, up and down the dunes. Matilda, my littlest, about 20 months old, was very determined in her running and found her way to a little dip in the side of the curve of the sand. She began to dance and sing and chant, an incantation. The adults on the ridge began to watch her.
Looks like she's playing with friends,
one said.
Invisible friends,
said another.
Ghost children,
said my mind.

And indeed it did, she was dancing, in a circle, holding hands, playing tag, all by herself as her sisters slid on the dunes. When it was time to go, her grief was immeasurable.
Wailing, weeping, pulling at her clothes, she ended up naked and running, free from my arms back to the dunes. Her fury when recaptured, her sobbing in the car and her absent eyes, were frightening.
I held her tight as she struggled, fear gripping my chest even as her hot, teary face, pulled away from my body. What if she never came back?
Ernie, the guide, had been watching all this.
We better do a smoking, you better bring her.
And so
as the gum leaves poured their oily, tear-stinging smoke into the sky, Matilda was held aloft, over the low burning fire, in the old Uncle's arms, until finally, she softened and nestled, against his chest
and the wild grief

seemed to leave her,
and she was cradled back to me.
She'll be alright now
Ernie said.
She'll be alright.

There is a humming sound and I realise that it is bees,
bees buzzing around the bins,
the bins filled with flowers. I pay attention, sit up straight in my plastic chair, try to look professional. Of course, I reflect, if I did take the flowers, who is to say that a ghost wouldn't follow me home? An angry little ghost, wild with me for raiding the bin.
I turn my body away from the light of the open roller door and back towards the oven. I can feel someone's eyes on me through the glass, another high-vis man, he wants me to give another nod, the final nod.
I nod.
He opens up the heavy metal oven door. This is no simple thing, it requires strength and levers and turnings of bolts, but the man is efficient and matter of fact and the door swings, slowly, open. I think I was expecting flames, Dante style, but the oven is simply steel and cool and grey.
The door opens.
I stand.
My hands open,
palms facing the coffin,
my back straightens,
tall now,
Spirit in me,
flowing out

of me,
like
a lighthouse
like
an
emptying.
I pray
I pray hard.
Like swimming.
I can feel the high-vis man's eyes still on me, he is waiting,
respectful, patient, maybe a bit bemused.
He wants me to give another nod,
the final nod.

I nod.

The coffin slides in, it's made secure, the door is shut.
The bolts slide back, into place.
My hands still outstretched.
Spirit through me, an emptying out, nothing of
'me'
left
Speak now.

Do not be afraid, my love...
Into the freedom of wind and sunshine... We will let you go.
Into the dance of the stars and the planets...We will let you go
Into the wind's breath and the hands of the star maker... We will let you go.

Later, as I get in my car,
I see a crow,
hopping,
next to the bin.
Crows, unlike most other creatures,
are 'gaze followers'.
This one looks me in the eye.
And holds my soul.
Till I shut the door
and drive away.

Sources

Crow by Ted Hughes published by Faber and Faber
'Grief is not the weather' taken with permission from
<u>WHY GRIEF IS LOVE – Stephen Jenkinson | London Real
YouTube·London Real</u>·7 June 2019

Acknowledgments

This book could not have made its way out into the world without the encouragement, kindness and calling forward by Georgia Richter and Hugh McGinlay.

Deep thanks also to the communion of old men minister saints and mentors: Peter Matheson, John Rickard and Alf Foote.

To the community that is Saint Andrew's – where many of these stories were found – it was an honour to be your minister for so many years. To the community at the Drop In – thanks for welcoming me in and letting me become part of the Hub.

To my sister, the writer.

To crow, my companion and my galvanising spirit bird.

To all those who have loved and lost – everything will be all right. And to the endlings – I am so sorry and, like a murmuration, we will rise, and we will not give up.

do they make coffins that small – a radio play.

do they make coffins that small can also be experienced as a short radio play.

Listen with headphones and be immersed or share in a small group for reflection and leaping off, into what it awakens in you...

do they make coffins that small

Directed by **Glynis Angel**

Come with me and watch bodies burn, stand by grave sites with blokes in High Vis
and get arrested outside mining camps far up in the outback..
Be broken.
Hold the hand of the man abused by the priest
and hang with a **crow**
who will act as your guide,
straddle the sacred and secular divide....

do they make coffins that small powerfully breaks open an ancient story of meaning making and invites you to hear the voice of

a god
and a ghost
and a black bird....